## The route to your roots

When they look back at their formative years, many Indians nostalgically recall the vital part Amar Chitra Katha picture books have played in their lives. It was **ACK – Amar Chitra Katha** – that first gave them a glimpse of their glorious heritage.

Since they were introduced in 1967, there are now **over 400 Amar Chitra Katha** titles to choose from. **Over 100 million copies** have been sold worldwide.

Now the Amar Chitra Katha titles are even more widely available in **1000+ bookstores all across India**. You can also buy all the titles through our online store **www.amarchitrakatha.com**. We provide quick delivery anywhere in the world.

To make it easy for you to locate the titles of your choice from our treasure trove of titles, the books are now arranged in five categories.

### Epics and Mythology
Best known stories from the Epics and the Puranas

### Indian Classics
Enchanting tales from Indian literature

### Fables and Humour
Evergreen folktales, legends and tales of wisdom and humour

### Bravehearts
Stirring tales of brave men and women of India

### Visionaries
Inspiring tales of thinkers, social reformers and nation builders

### Contemporary Classics
The Best of Modern Indian literature

D1733216

## Amar Chitra Katha Pvt Ltd
© Amar Chitra Katha Pvt Ltd, 1972, Reprinted September 2019,
ISBN 978-81-8482-172-7
Published by Amar Chitra Katha Pvt. Ltd., AFL House, 7th Floor,
Lok Bharati Complex,Marol Maroshi Road, Andheri (East), Mumbai - 400059, India.
For Consumer Complaints Contact Tel : + 91-2249188881/2
Email: customerservice@ack-media.com
Printed in India

This book is sold subject to the condition that the publication may not be reproduced,
stored in a retrieval system (including but not limited to computers, disks, external drives, electronic or digital devices, e-readers, websites),
or transmitted in any form or by any means (including but not limited to cyclostyling, photocopying, docutech or other reprographic reproductions,
mechanical, recording, electronic, digital versions) without the prior written permission of the publisher, nor be otherwise circulated in any form of
binding or cover other than that in which it is published and without a similar condition being imposed on the subsequent purchaser.

**The route to your roots**

# BIRD STORIES

The heroes of these tales value their friends, their families and their honour. They are brave and selfless. Though each one of them is a bird they are almost always exceptionally wise, at times cunning, and often blessed with a sense of humour – just the sort of role models people need to survive the workaday world.

**Script**
Kamala Chandrakant

**Illustrations**
Ashok Dongre

**Editor**
Anant Pai

*Cover illustration by: C.M. Vitankar*

# THE VALUE OF FRIENDS

LONG AGO, ON THE SHORE OF A LARGE LAKE, THERE LIVED A HAWK.

THEN ONE DAY, A SHE-HAWK CAME TO LIVE ON THE OPPOSITE SHORE. WHEN THE HAWK HEARD OF IT HE FLEW OVER TO HER.

WILL YOU BE MY WIFE? TOGETHER WE COULD RAISE A FINE FAMILY

ALL RIGHT. BUT TELL ME, DO YOU HAVE ANY FRIENDS?

NO.

THEN YOU MUST MAKE SOME FRIENDS. IN TIMES OF NEED, IT IS FRIENDS WHO HELP.

I DON'T NEED FRIENDS. BUT I'LL DO AS YOU SAY. WHO SHALL WE START WITH?

OUR NEIGHBOURS, OF COURSE! GO AND CALL ON THE LION, THE OSPREY AND THE TORTOISE!

THE HAWK AGREED AND FLEW TO THE TINY ISLAND IN THE MIDDLE OF THE LAKE WHERE THE TORTOISE DWELT.

O, TORTOISE, ACCEPT ME AS YOUR FRIEND.

WITH PLEASURE!

HE THEN MADE FRIENDS WITH THE OSPREY.

ANY TIME YOU NEED ME, SEND FOR ME.

FINALLY, THE HAWK CALLED ON THE LION—

NOW THAT YOU ARE MY FRIEND, NO ONE WILL HARM YOU.

THE HAWK THEN RETURNED TO THE SHE-HAWK.

I HAVE THREE FRIENDS NOW.

AH! NOW WE CAN DECIDE WHERE TO MAKE OUR HOME.

WHAT ABOUT THE KADAMBA TREE ON THE ISLAND WHERE THE TORTOISE LIVES?

THAT'S A GOOD IDEA.

SO THE TWO FLEW OVER TO THE ISLAND AND MADE A NEST ON THE KADAMBA TREE. SOON TWO LITTLE ONES WERE BORN TO THEM.

THIS IS THE SAFEST PLACE WE COULD FIND — FAR FROM THE HAUNTS OF MEN.

BUT THE PLACE WAS NOT AS SAFE AS THE HAWKS IMAGINED. ONE DAY TWO HUNTERS CAME —

IT'S BEEN A BAD DAY. WE'VE CAUGHT NOTHING, NOT EVEN A RABBIT!

AND IT'S ALMOST EVENING!

WE CAN'T RETURN EMPTY-HANDED!

WE MIGHT YET CATCH A FISH OR A YOUNG TORTOISE, PERHAPS.

BUT THEY HAD NO LUCK. TOWARDS NIGHTFALL —

WHAT SHALL WE DO?

LET'S SWIM ACROSS TO THAT ISLAND, AND SPEND THE NIGHT THERE. AT DAWN WE'LL TRY OUR LUCK AGAIN.

WHEN THEY REACHED THE ISLAND —

THESE MOSQUITOES ARE IMPOSSIBLE!

LET'S LIGHT A FIRE. THAT SHOULD DRIVE THEM AWAY.

CHEEP CHEEP

DID YOU HEAR THAT?

I DID! FLEDGLINGS! ON THIS TREE!

DID YOU HEAR THAT? HUMAN VOICES!

SH-S-SH! LET'S FIND OUT WHAT THEY ARE PLANNING.

THEY ARE PLANNING TO EAT OUR CHILDREN! FRIEND TORTOISE IS ASLEEP. QUICK, MY DEAR, FLY TO THE OSPREY AND SEEK HIS HELP.

THE OSPREY WAS SURPRISED TO SEE THE HAWK.

WHAT BRINGS YOU HERE AT THIS HOUR?

WHEN THE HAWK TOLD HIM —

HAVE THEY CLIMBED THE TREE YET?

NOT YET. THEY'RE BUSY LIGHTING A FIRE.

THEN FLY BACK TO YOUR WIFE AND COMFORT HER. I'LL TAKE CARE OF THE HUNTERS.

UNDER COVER OF NIGHT, THE OSPREY FLEW TO THE KADAMBA TREE AND WAITED AND WATCHED.

THERE! THE FIRE IS BLAZING MERRILY. LET'S GET THE BIRDS.

NOW TO PUT MY PLAN INTO ACTION!

SUDDENLY THE OSPREY DIVED INTO THE LAKE...

...CAME OUT, SHOOK HIMSELF OVER THE FIRE...

...AND PUT IT OUT.

HISSS

?

WHAT'S THAT? IS IT THE FIRE? PERHAPS, THE WOOD WAS WET!

COME DOWN. IT'S NO USE CATCHING THE FLEDGLINGS TILL THE FIRE IS ABLAZE AGAIN.

HISSS

THE HUNTERS SOON HAD ANOTHER FIRE BLAZING.

THERE! NOW LET'S BRING THEM DOWN.

BUT AS SOON AS THEY WENT TO GET THE BIRDS, THE OSPREY ONCE AGAIN PUT OUT THE FIRE.

THIS WENT ON TILL MIDNIGHT. THE SHE-HAWK FELT SORRY FOR THE OSPREY.

HE'LL LOSE HIS LIFE TRYING TO SAVE OUR YOUNG ONES. GO TO FRIEND TORTOISE AND SEE IF HE CAN HELP.

WHEN THE HAWK FLEW TO THE TORTOISE AND TOLD HIM THE WHOLE STORY—

DON'T WORRY. I'LL COME THERE AS QUICKLY AS I CAN.

SOON —

HEY, LOOK! A HUGE TORTOISE! LET'S FORGET THE BIRDS AND CATCH HIM. WE'LL HAVE ENOUGH FOOD FOR DAYS.

THEY TORE THEIR WAISTBANDS INTO STRIPS...

...AND BOUND THE TORTOISE TO THEIR BODIES.

NOW, PULL AWAY!

I WILL! I WILL! I'LL PULL YOU ALL RIGHT!

SUDDENLY —

HEY!

HELP!

THAT SHOULD TAKE CARE OF YOU.

THE HUNTERS QUICKLY LOOSENED THE STRIPS OF CLOTH THAT BOUND THEM TO THE TORTOISE.

THE FELLOW IS DANGEROUS! LET'S LEAVE HIM HERE AND MAKE ANOTHER FIRE FOR OUR FLEDGLINGS.

THEY BEGAN TO COLLECT TWIGS.

THEY'RE BACK! GO TO THE LION AND SEEK HIS HELP.

# GREED DOES NOT PAY

THERE ONCE WAS A BRAHMANA WHO HAD A WIFE AND THREE DAUGHTERS. HE LOVED THEM DEARLY AND TOOK GOOD CARE OF THEM.

THEN SUDDENLY ONE DAY HE DIED.

HOW COULD HE LEAVE US AND GO? WHO WILL CARE FOR US NOW?

SOME KIND NEIGHBOURS WHO HEARD HER WAILING RUSHED IN.

WE WILL. WE WON'T LET YOU STARVE. NOW PLEASE WIPE YOUR TEARS.

MEANWHILE, THE BRAHMANA WAS REBORN AS A GOLDEN SWAN. ONE DAY —

I MUST GO AND SEE HOW MY WIFE AND DAUGHTERS ARE GETTING ALONG.

HE PLUCKED OUT ONE OF HIS GOLDEN FEATHERS...

...GAVE IT TO HER...

...AND FLEW AWAY.

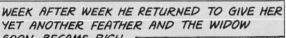

WEEK AFTER WEEK HE RETURNED TO GIVE HER YET ANOTHER FEATHER AND THE WIDOW SOON BECAME RICH.

BUT, ALAS! LIKE MOST RICH PEOPLE SHE BECAME GREEDY. ONE DAY —

SUPPOSE HE STOPS COMING? A MERE BIRD IS NOT TO BE TRUSTED.

THE NEXT TIME HE COMES, I'LL PLUCK OUT ALL HIS FEATHERS.

YOU CAN'T MEAN IT, MOTHER!

NO, MOTHER! YOU CAN'T DO THAT!

BUT THE WIDOW HAD MADE UP HER MIND. THE NEXT TIME THE BIRD CAME...

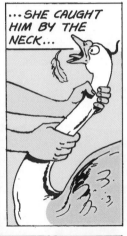

...SHE CAUGHT HIM BY THE NECK...

...AND DESPITE ALL HIS STRUGGLING, PLUCKED HIM CLEAN.

NOT ALL MY FEATHERS! NO! PLEASE DON'T! I...

THERE! NOW WE'LL NEVER BE POOR AGAIN!

ALAS! WHAT HAVE YOU DONE! TAKE A LOOK AT THE FEATHERS.

I'VE BEEN CHEATED! THEY'RE JUST ORDINARY WHITE FEATHERS! H-HOW DID IT HAPPEN?

I'LL TELL YOU HOW. MY GOLDEN FEATHERS TURNED WHITE BECAUSE YOU...YOU PLUCKED THEM AGAINST MY WILL. I FORGOT TO WARN YOU NEVER TO DO THAT.

YOU FORGOT ? HOW COULD YOU BE SO CARELESS ! WE ARE RUINED!

THAT'S WHERE A USELESS BIRD BELONGS ... THE DUSTBIN. ONE OF YOU GIVE HIM SOMETHING TO EAT.

WITHIN MONTHS, THE SWAN'S FEATHERS GREW AGAIN. BUT THEY WERE ALL WHITE.

WHAT'S THE USE OF STAYING ON HERE ? I'D BETTER GO AWAY.

AS FOR THE GREEDY WIFE SHE SOON FINISHED ALL HER MONEY AND FELL UPON BAD DAYS AS SHE WELL DESERVED.

# THE LOYAL GENERAL

LONG AGO IN VARANASI, THERE LIVED A KING CROW WHO HAD A MATE HE LOVED DEARLY.

ONE DAY, AS THEY FLEW PAST THE PALACE OF THE KING OF VARANASI, QUEEN CROW SAW A SIGHT WHICH MADE HER MOUTH WATER.

AH! HOW I WISH I COULD TASTE JUST A TINY BIT OF THAT FISH!

THE NEXT DAY —

COME, MY LOVE. LET'S GO OUT AND LOOK FOR SOME FOOD.

I DON'T WANT THE KIND OF FOOD WE FIND!

I WANT THE FOOD I SAW IN THE PALACE ON THE KING'S TABLE. IF I CAN'T HAVE IT, I'LL DIE.

AS THE KING CROW WONDERED WHAT HE SHOULD DO, HIS GENERAL CAME UP.

YOUR MAJESTY, WHAT'S THE MATTER?

WHEN THE KING CROW TOLD HIM—

OH! IS THAT ALL? DON'T WORRY. I'LL SEE THAT OUR QUEEN HAS THE FOOD SHE CRAVES FOR.

TAKING EIGHT OF THE BEST CROWS WITH HIM, THE GENERAL FLEW TOWARDS THE PALACE.

LET'S PERCH ON THE KITCHEN ROOF.

NOW LISTEN CAREFULLY. WHILE THE FOOD IS BEING TAKEN TO THE KING, I'LL MAKE THE COOK DROP THE DISHES.

FOUR OF YOU MUST THEN FILL YOUR BEAKS WITH RICE AND FOUR WITH FISH, AND FLY TO OUR QUEEN.

AH! HERE COMES THE COOK! WHEN HE REACHES THE OPEN COURTYARD, I'LL STRIKE!

THE NEXT MOMENT —

AIEEE!

AIEEEE!

DROP THOSE DISHES AND CATCH THAT WICKED CROW!

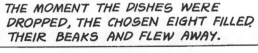

THE MOMENT THE DISHES WERE DROPPED, THE CHOSEN EIGHT FILLED THEIR BEAKS AND FLEW AWAY.

AH! THE QUEEN'S LONGING WILL BE SATISFIED. THEY CAN DO WHAT THEY WILL WITH ME, NOW.

GOOD! YOU'VE GOT HIM! BRING HIM HERE.

O, CROW! YOU HAVE DARED TO DISPLEASE ME. AND IN THIS FOOLISH VENTURE YOU'VE RISKED YOUR VERY LIFE! WHY DID YOU DO IT?

FOR MY KING. HE TOLD ME ABOUT THE QUEEN'S LONGING FOR THE FOOD SHE SAW ON YOUR TABLE. I PROMISED TO GET IT FOR HER — AND I HAVE KEPT MY PROMISE.

THE BIRD WAS WILLING TO SACRIFICE HIS LIFE FOR HIS KING! SUCH LOYALTY IS RARE! HE MUST BE REWARDED.

SET HIM FREE!

HENCEFORTH A PORTION OF THE FOOD COOKED FOR ME, SHALL BE SENT EVERY DAY TO YOU AND YOUR KING AND QUEEN. AND A LARGE MEASURE OF RICE SHALL BE COOKED FOR YOUR KING'S FOLLOWING.

# PRACTISE WHAT YOU PREACH

ONCE THE KING OF THE BIRDS TOOK HIS FLOCK TO THE HIMALAYAS IN SEARCH OF FOOD.

NOW GO AND LOOK FOR SEEDS AND GRAIN. WHEN YOU FIND SOME, REPORT TO ME, SO WE CAN ALL SHARE IT.

AS THEY WANDERED OFF, ONE OF THE BIRDS CAME TO A ROAD ALONG WHICH WAGONS LOADED WITH GRAIN USED TO PASS.

LOOK AT ALL THAT GRAIN ON THE ROAD. WHAT A FEAST! I WON'T TELL THE KING ABOUT THIS FIND!

BUT WHAT IF ONE OF THE OTHERS SHOULD FLY THIS WAY AND SEE THE GRAIN?

I KNOW! I'LL TELL THEM ABOUT IT AND YET KEEP THEM AWAY!

SHE FLEW BACK.

YOU'VE BEEN AWAY A LONG TIME! HAVE YOU HAD ANY LUCK?

NONE AT ALL! IN FACT, I VERY NEARLY LOST MY LIFE!

THE BIRDS WERE ALL EARS.

I HAPPENED TO FLY OVER THE HIGHWAY! ELEPHANTS AND HORSES, AND WAGONS DRAWN BY FIERCE BULLOCKS GO ALONG THAT ROUTE.

WAGONS? THEN THERE MUST BE PLENTY OF GRAIN THERE! AND...

THERE IS. BUT ONCE YOU ALIGHT IT'S DIFFICULT TO SOAR UP AGAIN. DON'T GO THAT WAY. IT'S DANGEROUS.

AFTER HER WARNING, THE OTHER BIRDS WERE CAREFUL TO AVOID THE HIGHWAY.

THAT WAS CLEVER OF ME! I HAVE ALL THIS GRAIN TO MYSELF NOW.

SUDDENLY —

WHRRRR

WHAT'S THAT? OH! A CART!

IT'S A LONG WAY OFF. THERE'S ENOUGH TIME TO PECK A FEW MORE SEEDS.

WHRRR

WHAT SHE DIDN'T KNOW WAS THAT IT WAS AN EXPRESS CART.

WHRrrr

WHRRRR

SUDDENLY —

OH! NO! IT'S ALMOST UPON ME!

BUT BEFORE SHE COULD TAKE WING, THE CART RAN OVER HER.

WHRrrr

THAT EVENING, WHEN ALL THE BIRDS CAME HOME TO ROOST, THEY FOUND HER MISSING.

GO AND LOOK FOR HER.

THE BIRDS FLEW IN ALL DIRECTIONS IN SEARCH OF THEIR LOST COMPANION.

LATER, A FEW BIRDS REPORTED TO THE KING —

SHE'S DEAD!

WE FOUND HER ON THE HIGHWAY.... A CART MUST HAVE RUN OVER HER.

THE KING FLEW TO THE SPOT AT ONCE.

WHAT A SAD FATE! SHE WARNED YOU NOT TO GO NEAR THE HIGHWAY. BUT SHE COULD NOT CONTROL HER OWN GREED. LET THIS BE A LESSON TO ALL OF YOU!

# THE GREEDY CROW

A PIGEON ONCE MADE ITS HOME IN THE KITCHEN OF A RICH MERCHANT OF VARANASI.

ONE DAY, A GREEDY CROW FLEW PAST.

MM-M! FISH! I MUST FIND MY WAY INTO THIS KITCHEN AND MAKE IT MY HOME. BUT HOW SHOULD I GO ABOUT IT?

JUST THEN HIS EYE FELL ON THE PIGEON.

I'VE GOT IT! I'LL MAKE FRIENDS WITH HIM!

AS THE PIGEON FLEW OUT IN SEARCH OF FOOD, THE CROW FOLLOWED HIM. AFTER A WHILE—

WHY DO YOU FOLLOW ME, FRIEND?

I LIKE YOU. I WOULD LIKE TO FEED WITH YOU.

AND SO THE CROW, TOO, BEGAN TO LIVE IN THE KITCHEN. THEN, ONE EVENING AS THE TWO RETURNED HOME —

THE MASTER IS HAVING A BANQUET TOMORROW. CLEAN AND CUT ALL THIS FISH TONIGHT.

LOOK AT HIS MOUTH WATER!

WHAT LUCK! I'VE ALREADY EATEN MY FILL TODAY. TOMORROW I'LL FEAST — NOT ON WORMS BUT ON FISH!

THAT NIGHT —

AA-A-AH! OO-OH!

WHAT'S THE MATTER WITH YOU?

I DON'T KNOW! IT MUST BE THE WORMS I ATE TODAY!

OR IS IT THE FISH YOU WANT TO EAT TOMORROW?

THE NEXT MORNING —

COME ON, LET'S GO.

I'M NOT COMING TODAY. YOU GO ALONE. I HAVE A TERRIBLE STOMACHACHE.

NONSENSE! IT'S THE FISH, ISN'T IT? TAKE MY ADVICE. IT IS DANGEROUS TO TOUCH MEN'S FOOD. COME, LET'S GO. UP WITH YOU!

WHAT! AND GIVE UP WHAT I CAME HERE FOR IN THE FIRST PLACE! NEVER!

I DO HAVE A STOMACHACHE. YOU GO.

ALL RIGHT, I'M GOING. BUT TAKE CARE.

AS THE PIGEON FLEW OUT, THE COOK ENTERED AND SET TO WORK.

THESE PIECES I'LL FRY. AND THESE I'LL PUT INTO THE CURRY.

AH! THE BEST BITS ARE TO BE FRIED! I'LL SETTLE FOR FRIED FISH!

WHEN THE FOOD WAS READY, THE COOK COVERED THE DISHES.

I'LL GO OUT AND REST FOR A WHILE TILL THE MAID COMES FOR THE FOOD.

IT IS HIGH TIME YOU WENT OUT. I CANNOT WAIT ANY LONGER.

YOU THIEF! IS THIS HOW YOU REPAY ME FOR SHELTERING YOU?

BEFORE THE STARTLED CROW COULD REALISE WHAT WAS HAPPENING, THE COOK POUNCED ON HIM.

I'LL PLUCK YOU CLEAN AND SOAK YOU IN A MIXTURE OF SOUR BUTTERMILK AND SPICES!

LATER —

O-O-OH! A-A-AH!

THAT SHOULD TEACH YOU NEVER TO BE GREEDY AGAIN!

THAT EVENING WHEN THE PIGEON FLEW IN AND SAW THE CROW'S PLIGHT —

ALAS, MY GREEDY FRIEND IF ONLY YOU HAD LISTENED TO ME!

# SEVEN KANDS!
## One Legendary Tale!

VALMIKI'S RAMAYANA

## TAKE AN EPIC JOURNEY
## FROM AYODHYA TO LANKA AND BACK!

BUY ONLINE ON WWW.AMARCHITRAKATHA.COM

# Explore fascinating
# INDIAN FOLKLORE
from every nook and corner of the country

Buy online on
## www.amarchitrakatha.com

# 21 Inspiring
# Stories of Courage

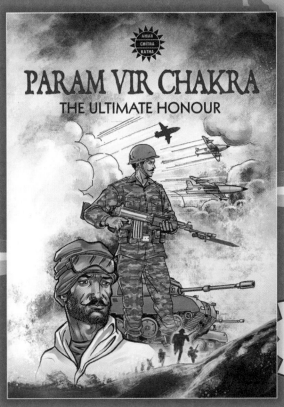

**MRP ₹399/-**

To buy this product, visit your nearest bookstore
or buy online at **www.amarchitrakatha.com** or call: **022-49188881/2**

# Amar Chitra Katha's

# EXCITING STORY CATEGORIES, ONE AMAZING DESTINATION.

From the episodes of Mahabharata to the wit of Birbal,
from the valour of Shivaji to the teachings of Tagore,
from the adventures of Pratapan to the tales of Ruskin Bond –
Amar Chitra Katha stories span across different genres to get you the best of literature.

To buy/view our products go to
**www.amarchitrakatha.com**

AMAR
CHITRA
KATHA

# MONKEY STORIES

### JATAKA TALES OF WILE AND WISDOM

**The route to your roots**

# MONKEY STORIES

Monkeys frolic through these pages, imparting lessons in leadership and common sense. Murderous crocodiles, powerful kings and fearsome ogres are easily outwitted by these winsome creatures. All they seem to need is careful thought and a lot of courage. But be warned: do not let monkeys loose in your garden or you may well lose sight of their virtues!

**Script**
Meena Talim

**Illustrations**
Jeffrey Fowler

**Editor**
Anant Pai

# ★ THE MONKEY KING'S SACRIFICE

FRIENDS! WE HAVE BEEN LIVING HAPPILY ON THIS MANGO TREE FOR YEARS.

BUT I ANTICIPATE TROUBLE, SOON.

WHY MASTER?

MEN HAVE COME TO LIVE NEAR OUR FOREST. THEY HAVE NEVER TASTED THE MANGO FRUIT.

1

★ BASED ON MAHA KAPI JATAKA

ONCE THEY DO, IT WILL BE DANGEROUS FOR US.

OH DEAR! WHAT SHALL WE DO?

MAKE SURE THAT NOT A SINGLE FRUIT FALLS INTO THE RIVER.

PLUCK EACH AND EVERY BUD FROM THE BRANCHES THAT SPREAD OUT OVER THE RIVER.

BUT IN SPITE OF ALL THIS CARE, A JUICY RIPE MANGO FELL INTO THE RIVER...

SPLAT

... AND GOT CAUGHT IN A FISHERMAN'S NET.

2

THEY WERE LET IN.

OH MASTER, THIS FRUIT WAS AMONG THE FISH I CAUGHT.

HM-M!

SEND FOR THE FORESTER. HE WILL TELL US WHAT FRUIT IT IS.

THAT'S THE RARE MANGO, SIR.

IS IT POISONOUS?

NOT AT ALL, SIR. IN FACT IT IS VERY TASTY.

SO THE KING SUNK HIS TEETH INTO IT.

HM-M-M! DELICIOUS.

IT SMELLS GOOD, TOO!

NEXT MORNING —

TELL ME FORESTER, WHERE DOES THIS MANGO FRUIT GROW.

THERE IS A MANGO GROVE, JUST A LITTLE UPSTREAM, SIR.

MINISTER, MAKE THE NECESSARY ARRANGEMENTS. WE ARE LEAVING FOR THAT GROVE.

YES, SIR.

SOON THEY WERE OFF.

I HOPE YOU HAVE BROUGHT SOME ARCHERS ALONG.

I HAVE, SIR.

WHEN THEY REACHED THE SPOT —

TELL EVERYONE TO EAT AS MUCH AS THEY CAN.

MINISTER, WE WILL STAY HERE FOR A DAY OR TWO.

I WILL MAKE THE ARRANGEMENTS, SIR.

AS NIGHT FELL, THE MONKEYS BEGAN MOVING ABOUT.

MINISTER, WHAT WAS THAT?

JUST MONKEYS SIR, SCAMPERING AMONG THE BRANCHES.

WHEN IT'S MORNING, TELL THE ARCHERS TO SHOOT EVERY SINGLE MONKEY.

I SHALL, SIR.

THE NEXT MORNING—

TODAY ALONG WITH THE MANGOES WE SHALL EAT MONKEY'S FLESH.

OH MASTER, WE'RE TRAPPED.

WHAT ARE WE TO DO NOW?

EYOW

DON'T PANIC. I'LL FIND A WAY OUT.

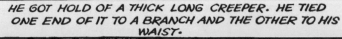

THEY MANAGED TO GET TO A TREE NEAR THE RIVER.

NOW ALL OF YOU DO AS I TELL YOU.

HE GOT HOLD OF A THICK LONG CREEPER. HE TIED ONE END OF IT TO A BRANCH AND THE OTHER TO HIS WAIST.

NOW I WILL SWING OVER THE RIVER TO THAT FIG TREE ON THE OPPOSITE BANK. ONE BY ONE YOU CAN COME ACROSS TO THE OTHER SIDE.

OH NO! THE VINE IS TOO SHORT.

I WILL TRY TO GET HOLD OF THIS BRANCH AND BRIDGE THE GAP.

# ★THE STUPID CROCODILE AND THE MONKEY

IN A DENSE JUNGLE, NEAR A RIVER, THERE LIVED A CLEVER LITTLE MONKEY.

HM! I'M HUNGRY.

IN THE MIDDLE OF THE RIVER WAS A SMALL ISLAND, WHERE PLENTY OF DELICIOUS FRUITS GREW. WHENEVER THE MONKEY FELT HUNGRY, HE WENT STRAIGHT TO THE ISLAND.

★ BASED ON VANARINDA JATAKA

HE WOULD JUMP FROM THE BANK, ONTO A ROCK IN THE RIVER AND THEN TO THE SMALL ISLAND.

BREAKFAST. HERE I COME!

HMM! NOTHING LIKE FRUIT FOR A HEALTHY BREAKFAST.

HUH...

?

PUCH

ROTTEN FRUIT!

I WONDER WHERE IT CAME FROM.

PUCH

OH WELL! ONE MUST TAKE THE GOOD WITH THE BAD!

THE NEXT DAY AS USUAL THE MONKEY SET OUT FOR THE ISLAND.

I'M HUNGRY!

SO AM I! HEE! HEE!

WHEN HE HAD EATEN TO HIS STOMACH'S CONTENT—

HEY! THAT'S STRANGE! THAT ROCK LOOKS BIGGER TODAY.

THE RIVER HAS NOT GONE DRY FOR IT TO LOOK BIGGER.

I'M SURE IT IS THAT STUPID CROCODILE, UP TO HIS TRICKS AGAIN. I WON'T JUMP TILL I'M SURE.

LET ME SEE IF THIS IDEA WORKS.

HELLO ROCK! HOW ARE YOU TODAY, MY FRIEND?

THE MONKEY CALLED OVER AND OVER AGAIN.

WHY AREN'T YOU SPEAKING TO ME TODAY ROCK? HAVE I ANNOYED YOU?

IT LOOKS AS IF THIS ROCK USED TO TALK TO HIM. I'D BETTER REPLY.

AS THE MONKEY HAD EXPECTED, THE MOMENT THE CROCODILE OPENED HIS MOUTH WIDE, HIS EYES CLOSED.

NOW'S MY CHANCE. I'LL JUMP ON HIM AND ONTO THE BANK. I'LL HAVE TO BE QUICK.

TAKE THAT!

THUD

WHAT WAS THAT?

WHAT ARE YOU DOING OVER THERE? YOU PROMISED YOU WOULD JUMP INTO MY MOUTH.

DID YOU REALLY BELIEVE I'D DO A STUPID THING LIKE THAT?

GRR! WAIT TILL I GET MY TEETH INTO YOU.

YOU NEVER WILL, CROCODILE. YOU MAY BE BIG AND STRONG BUT YOU ARE STUPID.

# ★THE DEMON OUTWITTED

LONG AGO A BAND OF MONKEYS CAME AND SETTLED ON THE OUTSKIRTS OF A FOREST.

THE LEADER WHO KNEW THE PLACE WELL, CALLED A MEETING.

ATTENTION, ALL OF YOU! I HAVE SOMETHING IMPORTANT TO SAY.

YOU WILL HAVE TO BE CAREFUL ABOUT TWO THINGS IN THIS FOREST.

THERE ARE CERTAIN POISONOUS TREES WITH VERY TEMPTING FRUIT AND ONE OF THE LAKES IS HAUNTED BY A DEMON.

★ BASED ON NALAPANA JATAKA

YOU MUST NOT DRINK WATER OR EAT ANY FRUIT WITHOUT ASKING ME.

ONE DAY WHILE SEARCHING FOR FIREWOOD, THE MONKEYS WANDERED DEEP INTO THE FOREST.

MOTHER, I'M THIRSTY.

AH! THERE IS A LAKE CLOSE BY.

WAIT! DON'T GO NEAR THE WATER.

DON'T YOU REMEMBER OUR LEADER'S WARNING?

OH DEAR! I'D COMPLETELY FORGOTTEN. THANK YOU FOR REMINDING ME.

ALL RIGHT! LET US WAIT TILL OUR LEADER COMES.

21

COLLECT ALL THE BAMBOO REEDS YOU CAN.

HM..M...M... THIS ONE'S FINE. ABSOLUTELY HOLLOW.

WHAT ABOUT THIS ONE?

EXCELLENT. IT FITS INTO THE OTHER PERFECTLY.

THUS BY JOINING A NUMBER OF THE REEDS TOGETHER THE LEADER MADE ONE LONG HOLLOW REED.

NOW I'LL SLIDE THAT END INTO THE WATER.

NOW WHAT?

I'LL SUCK THE WATER FROM THIS END.

AND WITH ALL HIS MIGHT HE SUCKED AT THE REED TILL...

SKURRRRR

...THE WATER GUSHED OUT IN A THICK STREAM.

SPLAT

WATER! DELICIOUS WATER! AND ALL FOR US.

FULL OF RAGE, THE OUTWITTED DEMON STOMPED BACK INTO THE LAKE.

GRRRR!

HA HA HA HO HO HEE HO HA HA

AND THE MONKEYS THEIR THIRST WELL QUENCHED, RETURNED HOME.

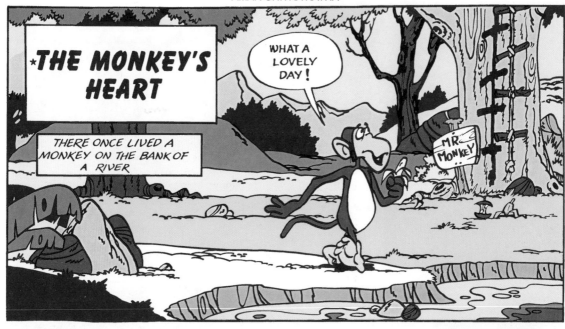

★THE MONKEY'S HEART

THERE ONCE LIVED A MONKEY ON THE BANK OF A RIVER

WHAT A LOVELY DAY!

MR. MONKEY

A LITTLE DOWNSTREAM LIVED A CROCODILE AND HIS WIFE.

HAVE YOU SEEN THAT PLUMP MONKEY UPSTREAM? I'M LONGING TO EAT HIS HEART.

I WOULD LOVE TO GET IT FOR YOU. BUT HE LIVES UP IN THE TREES. HOW CAN I CATCH HIM?

YOU ARE A CROCODILE, AREN'T YOU? USE YOUR CUNNING.

HUMM! LET'S SEE. MY IDEA MIGHT JUST WORK.

★ BASED ON SUMSUMARA JATAKA

## ★ THE MONKEYS AND THE GARDENER

THE KING OF VARANASI HAD A BEAUTIFUL GARDEN, WHICH WAS LOOKED AFTER BY A LOYAL GARDENER.

ONE NIGHT —

HELLO FRIEND. THE FESTIVAL IN TOWN BEGINS TOMORROW.

I KNOW!

THERE'S GOING TO BE PLENTY OF FUN.

HOW I WISH I COULD COME!

WHAT! AREN'T YOU COMING?

IF I DO, WHO WILL WATER THE GARDEN?

28

★ BASED ON ARMADUSAKA JATAKA

THE NEXT DAY—

WHY DO YOU LOOK SO SAD, GARDENER?

THERE'S A FESTIVAL ON IN TOWN.

WELL?

I WANT TO GO TO IT. BUT WHO WILL WATER MY GARDEN?

POOH! THAT'S NO PROBLEM.

MY FRIENDS AND I WILL WATER THE GARDEN FOR YOU.

YOU WILL?

THANK YOU, DEAR MONKEY. I'LL RETURN IN A FEW DAYS, AS SOON AS POSSIBLE

HAVE A FINE TIME, FRIEND.

NOW TO ROUND UP ALL MY FRIENDS!

COME ON, MY MONKEYS. WE HAVE WORK TO DO. VERY IMPORTANT WORK!

WHAT IS IT? WHAT DO WE HAVE TO DO?

THE GARDENER WANTS US TO WATER HIS GARDEN WHILE HE IS AWAY.

WHAT FUN!

WHEN CAN WE START?

RIGHT AWAY! GO GET THE WATERING CANS AND BUCKETS.

AS SOON AS THEY WERE READY—

SOME TREES ARE SMALL AND SOME ARE BIG!

THAT'S RIGHT! HOW MUCH WATER SHOULD WE GIVE TO EACH TREE?

THAT'S NO PROBLEM AT ALL.

MEANWHILE IN TOWN —

I WONDER HOW MY MONKEY FRIENDS ARE GETTING ALONG WITH THEIR TASK?

TWO DAYS LATER THE GARDENER RETURNED HOME.

WHAT HAVE YOU DONE?

WE WATERED EACH PLANT ACCORDING TO THE NEEDS OF ITS ROOTS

THAT'S RIGHT. WE DID.

WHATEVER, SHALL I DO NOW? WHAT SHALL I TELL THE KING?

THAT'S WHAT COMES OF DEPENDING ON A FOOL. HE MAY MEAN WELL BUT WILL END UP DOING MORE HARM THAN ANYTHING ELSE.

# DEER STORIES

## THE GENTLE WISDOM OF THE JATAKA

**The route to your roots**

# DEER STORIES

Deer, in the Jataka tales, are often gentle bodhisattvas or Buddhas-to-be. They are noble, selfless, wise and virtuous. As models of right thinking and right living, they strongly advise a life of non-violence and peace for ultimate happiness. Even if greed leads them astray, they are soon guided back to the correct path.

**Script**
The Editorial Team

**Illustrations**
Jeffrey Fowler

**Editor**
Anant Pai

**TRUE FRIENDSHIP**

IN A THICKET NEAR A LAKE, LIVED THREE FRIENDS, A TORTOISE, A WOODPECKER AND AN *ANTELOPE.

ONE DAY A HUNTER CAME THAT WAY.

AH! FOOTPRINTS! I'LL SET THE TRAP RIGHT HERE.

HE IS BOUND TO PASS THIS WAY TO DRINK WATER.

I'LL COME BACK FOR HIM TOMORROW.

AT DAWN—

IT'S GOOD TO BE ALIVE. I MUST HAVE A DRINK.

HELP!!

THE TORTOISE AND THE WOODPECKER HEARD HIS CRIES AND RUSHED TO HIM.

I'LL TELL YOU WHAT — YOU HAVE STRONG TEETH. YOU FREE HIM WHILE I KEEP THE HUNTER AWAY.

WHEN HE COMES OUT OF HIS HUT, I'LL GIVE HIM A GOOD PECKING.

THE TORTOISE WAS AS SLOW AS A TORTOISE COULD BE.

WILL YOU PLEASE HURRY.

MEANWHILE THE HUNTER TOO HAD HEARD THE ANTELOPE'S SHOUTS FOR HELP AND HAD RUSHED OUT.

SLAM

AH...AH, HE'S CAUGHT.

THE WOODPECKER SPIED HIM.

ZOOM

EYOOW

CRACK

SCREEEEEEEECH!!

I'D BETTER GET INDOORS.

PUFF PANT PUFF

I'VE GOT IT, I'LL TRY TO GO OUT BY THE BACK DOOR.

BUT—

I BET HE WILL TRY TO GET OUT FROM THE BACK DOOR.

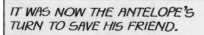

IT WAS NOW THE ANTELOPE'S TURN TO SAVE HIS FRIEND.

IF HE SEES ME, HE WILL CHASE ME, AND MY FRIEND CAN ESCAPE.

THE ANTELOPE SHOWED HIMSELF.

THERE GOES MY ANTELOPE.

THE HUNTER DROPPED HIS SACK AND RAN AFTER THE ANTELOPE.

I'LL LEAD HIM INTO MY FAVOURITE OLD CAVE.

ONCE HE IS IN HE WILL NOT KNOW HOW TO GET OUT.

WHAT A FOOL! HE'LL BE TRAPPED IN THE CAVE. HE'S DONE FOR.

HUH — WHERE DID HE GO?

I HOPE, FRIEND TORTOISE IS SAFE.

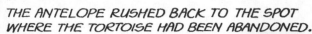

THE ANTELOPE RUSHED BACK TO THE SPOT WHERE THE TORTOISE HAD BEEN ABANDONED.

DON'T WORRY, MY FRIEND, I'LL SOON GET YOU OUT OF THE BAG!

MUFF MUFF

WHEN THE ANTELOPE LET THE TORTOISE OUT, THE WOODPECKER CAME DOWN FROM THE TREE.

WHAT HAPPENED TO THE HUNTER?

HA! HA! HA! HE IS RUNNING AROUND IN CIRCLES IN OUR OLD CAVE!

the End.

# *RURU, THE GOLDEN DEER

MAHADHANAKA WAS THE SON OF A RICH MERCHANT OF VARANASI. HIS FATHER, INSTEAD OF SENDING HIM TO SCHOOL, SPOILT HIM WITH ALL THE PLEASURES OF THE WORLD.

ENJOY YOURSELF, MY SON! I CAN GIVE YOU EVERYTHING.

I KNOW, FATHER!

WHEN HE CAME OF AGE, MAHADHANAKA WAS MARRIED TO A BEAUTIFUL GIRL.

YOUR MOTHER HAS COOKED THIS FOR YOU, MY LORD.

HM...M...M, IT SMELLS DELICIOUS!

SOON HIS PARENTS DIED AND HE WAS LEFT ALONE.

ALAS! WHO WILL LOOK AFTER ME NOW?

HIS FRIENDS WERE AFTER HIS MONEY.

COME ON MAHADHANAKA, CHEER UP. LET US HAVE A GAME OF DICE AND SOME WINE TO WARM US UP.

YES, THAT'S A GOOD IDEA.

\* Based on Ruru Jataka

MAHADHANAKA HAD NEVER HANDLED MONEY BEFORE, SO HE DID NOT KNOW HOW TO USE IT.

USE THE MOST EXPENSIVE CLOTH YOU HAVE, FOR OUR CLOTHES.

I CERTAINLY WILL, SIR.

LET US HAVE SOME MORE LIQUOR AND PLAY ANOTHER ROUND OF CARDS.

ONE DAY—

WHAT! NO MONEY! IF I DON'T DO SOMETHING I'LL SOON HAVE NO FRIENDS EITHER.

YES, THAT'S IT. I'LL BORROW SOME MONEY AND PAY IT BACK LATER.

HE WENT FROM ONE MONEY-LENDER TO ANOTHER AND PROMISED THEM THE SAME THING.

I'LL RETURN YOUR MONEY AS SOON AS I BECOME RICH AGAIN.

9

MONTHS PASSED. WHEN MAHADHANAKA SHOWED NO SIGN OF RETURNING THE MONEY—

YOU HAD BETTER PAY UP SOON, MAHADHANAKA, OR ELSE...

HAVE PATIENCE. I WILL.

BUT HE KNEW HE WOULD NEVER BE ABLE TO REPAY THE MONEY. AT LAST—

I WOULD RATHER DIE THAN FACE THE MONEY-LENDERS.

THEN ONE DAY MAHADHANAKA LED ALL HIS CREDITORS TO THE BANK OF A RIVER.

WHERE ARE YOU LEADING US?

I HAVE SOME TREASURE HIDDEN IN THE RIVER BED. I WILL RETURN ALL THAT I HAVE BORROWED FROM YOU.

NOW IS MY CHANCE TO SLIP AWAY, AND DROWN MYSELF. THAT WILL BE THE END TO ALL MY SORROWS.

SPLASH!

HELP! GLUB! GASP! HELP!

THAT NIGHT KHEMA, THE QUEEN OF VARANASI, HAD A DREAM.

SHE WOKE UP THE KING.

WHAT IS IT, MY QUEEN?

I DREAMT THAT A GOLDEN DEER PREACHED DHARMA TO ME. IF SUCH A DEER EXISTS, I WOULD LIKE TO HEAR ITS DISCOURSE.

IF THERE IS SUCH AN ANIMAL, YOU WILL.

THE KING SENT FOR HIS COUNCILLORS.

ARE THERE SUCH ANIMALS AS GOLDEN DEER?

YES, YOUR MAJESTY. THERE ARE.

I SHALL GIVE A REWARD TO THE MAN WHO CAN FIND ONE FOR ME.

THE REWARD WAS A SACK OF GOLD COINS PLACED IN A GOLD POT ON AN ELEPHANT'S BACK.

5

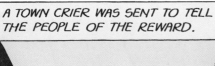

A TOWN CRIER WAS SENT TO TELL THE PEOPLE OF THE REWARD.

JUST THEN MAHADHANAKA STROLLED BY.

WHAT DID YOU SAY, MY FRIEND?

THE KING IS OFFERING A LARGE REWARD TO ANY MAN WHO CAN TELL HIM OF THE WHEREABOUTS OF A GOLDEN DEER.

HMMMM, I SHALL SOON BE RICH AGAIN.

TAKE ME TO THE KING.

SO HE WENT WITH THE COURTIER TO THE PALACE.

YOUR MAJESTY, THIS MAN SAYS HE KNOWS WHERE A GOLDEN DEER MAY BE FOUND.

HMMM!

IS THAT SO? WHEN CAN YOU LEAD US TO HIM.

AT THE BREAK OF DAWN, YOUR MAJESTY.

AT DAWN—

I HOPE YOU KNOW THE WAY.

THERE, YOUR MAJESTY, IN THAT GROVE OF MANGO AND SAL TREES, LIVES THE GOLDEN DEER YOU WANT.

SURROUND THE GROVE.

I'LL STAND A LITTLE WAY OFF AND SEE WHAT HAPPENS.

TIP TOE

WHEN THE DEER HEARD THE NOISE OF THE BEATERS—

THAT'S A HUNTING PARTY, I'M SURE. HOW DID THEY FIND THIS GROVE?

CLANG "THUMP"

PUT DOWN YOUR BOW, O KING. I'VE SOMETHING TO ASK YOU.

THE KING WAS ASTONISHED TO HEAR RURU'S VOICE.

I PROMISE I WON'T SHOOT. COME OUT OF YOUR HIDING PLACE.

WHAT IS IT YOU WANT TO KNOW?

YOUR MAJESTY, WHO TOLD YOU ABOUT ME AND WHERE I LIVE?

HE DID.

I THOUGHT AS MUCH. IT WOULD HAVE BEEN BETTER TO SAVE A LOG OF WOOD THAN A MAN LIKE HIM.

? WHAT DO YOU MEAN BY THAT?

YOUR MAJESTY, I ONCE SAVED THIS MAN FROM DROWNING, AND THIS IS HOW HE HAS REPAID ME.

IS THAT SO? HE SHALL BE HANGED FOR IT.

NO, DON'T DO THAT. I DON'T WANT HIM TO DIE BECAUSE OF ME.

YOU ARE LUCKY. BUT FOR HIM I WOULD HAVE HAD YOU HANGED. NOW GO AWAY.

THE KING THEN TURNED TO RURU.

ASK FOR ANYTHING, AND I'LL GRANT IT TO YOU.

YOUR MAJESTY, FROM NOW ON, LET NO ANIMAL OR BIRD BE HARMED BY ANYONE IN YOUR KINGDOM.

THEN THE KING IMMEDIATELY SENT AROUND A PROCLAMATION.

NO LIVING CREATURE BIG OR SMALL SHALL HENCE-FORTH BE HARMED. SHOULD ANYONE HARM THEM HE SHALL BE SEVERELY PUNISHED.

RURU THEN WENT WITH THE KING TO THE PALACE, DISCOURSED TO THE QUEEN AND RETURNED TO THE FOREST.

the End.

## THE HUNTER OUTWITTED

BROTHER, WILL YOU TEACH YOUR NEPHEW THE TRICKS OF OUR HERD?

CERTAINLY.

THERE ONCE LIVED A STAG IN THE FOREST NEAR RAJAGRIHA. ONE DAY HIS SISTER CAME TO HIM WITH HER SON.

GO HOME NOW, MY BOY, AND COME BACK TOMORROW.

NEXT DAY—

I WONDER WHAT UNCLE WILL TEACH ME.

EVERY DAY FOR TWO MONTHS THE LITTLE DEER WENT TO HIS UNCLE.

ONE DAY WHILE WANDERING THROUGH THE FOREST WITH HIS FRIENDS...

...HE STEPPED INTO A TRAP.

A..A..AH!

CLACK

HELP! I'M CAUGHT.

LET'S GO BACK AND TELL HIS MOTHER.

YOUR SON HAS BEEN CAUGHT IN A HUNTER'S TRAP.

OH DEAR, WHAT SHALL I DO?

SHE HURRIED TO THE STAG.

BROTHER, PLEASE HELP ME. MY SON HAS BEEN TRAPPED.

DO NOT FEAR, MY SISTER.

I HAVE NOT TAUGHT HIM FOR NOTHING. HE WILL RETURN. HAVE PATIENCE.

MEANWHILE—

I MUST REMEMBER WHAT UNCLE TAUGHT ME.

*HE OPENED THE TRAP.*

I'LL CUT HIM UP AND TAKE THE FLESH HOME. MY WIFE WILL BE PLEASED.

ON SECOND THOUGHTS I'LL ROAST SOME OF THE FLESH AND EAT IT HERE.

*AS HE WENT TO COLLECT SOME WOOD TO MAKE A FIRE—*

HEE..HEE... HEE...

HA...HA... HA...

COME BACK! COME BACK!

MY SON, YOU ARE BACK. HOW DID YOU ESCAPE?

HE WAS A GOOD STUDENT!

the End.

# *CAUTION PAYS

IN A FOREST NEAR VARANASI, THERE LIVED AN ANTELOPE WHICH WAS VERY FOND OF THE FRUITS OF A PARTICULAR TREE.

IN A VILLAGE NEAR BY LIVED A HUNTER, WHO KNEW THIS.

I MUST GET HIM TODAY.

EARLY THAT MORNING THE HUNTER WENT TO THE JUNGLE.

HMM. HE IS A BIG ANIMAL. I WILL GET QUITE SOME MONEY BY SELLING HIS MEAT.

HE PUT UP A *MACHAN ON THE TREE...

...AND WAITED FOR THE ANTELOPE.

HE SHOULD BE HERE ANY MOMENT.

AS USUAL THE ANTELOPE CAME STROL-LING ALONG.

MM..M..M. JUST THINKING OF THAT FRUIT MAKES ME HUNGRY.

HE WAS A CLEVER ANTELOPE AND NEVER MISSED A THING.

HEY! A MAN'S FOOTPRINTS!

THERE MUST BE A HUNTER NEAR BY, WAITING TO KILL ME.

WHY DOESN'T HE COME NEAR? I SHALL TRY THROWING SOME FRUIT TO HIM. MAYBE THAT WILL LURE HIM TO THE TREE.

OH OH, THERE IS SOMEONE UP THE TREE. THE FRUIT IS BEING THROWN TO ME. IT ISN'T DROP-PING AS IT USUALLY DOES.

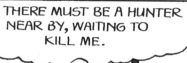

YES. NOW I AM SURE. I CAN SEE THE CORNER OF A 'MACHAN'.

# *THE GOLDEN ANTELOPE

LONG AGO THERE LIVED A KING IN VARANASI WHO HAD A GARDENER NAMED SANJAYA. EVERY DAY AN ANTELOPE CAME TO GRAZE IN THE ROYAL GARDEN.

POOR ANTELOPE! EVERY TIME HE SEES ME HE RUNS AWAY IN FRIGHT.

AFTER SOME TIME THE ANTELOPE BECAME ACCUSTOMED TO SEEING SANJAYA ABOUT AND STOPPED RUNNING AWAY.

ONE DAY WHILE HE WAS TAKING FRUIT AND FLOWERS TO THE PALACE, THE KING STOPPED HIM.

HAVE YOU NOTICED ANYTHING STRANGE IN THE GARDEN, SANJAYA?

NOTHING, YOUR MAJESTY, EXCEPT THAT A WILD ANTELOPE COMES TO GRAZE HERE FROM TIME TO TIME.

DO YOU THINK YOU COULD CATCH HIM?

OH YES. IF I HAD A LITTLE HONEY I WOULD BRING HIM RIGHT INTO YOUR PALACE.

* Based on Vatar Miga Jataka

24

THE KING ORDERED SOME HONEY TO BE GIVEN TO SANJAYA.

I SHALL COAT THE GRASS WHERE HE GRAZES WITH HONEY, THEN HIDE MYSELF AND SEE WHAT HAPPENS.

ALONG CAME THE ANTELOPE.

HMM. THIS GRASS TASTES EXCEPTIONALLY SWEET TODAY.

SO MY PLAN HAS WORKED. NOW FOR THE SECOND STAGE. HEE HEE.

THE ANTELOPE WAS SO SNARED BY THE TASTE OF THE SWEETENED GRASS, HE WOULD EAT NOWHERE ELSE.

HMM. NOW TO SHOW MYSELF GRADUALLY.

AT FIRST THE ANTELOPE WAS STARTLED AT THE APPEARANCE OF SANJAYA.

HUH?

BUT SOON HE WAS EATING THE SWEET GRASS THAT SANJAYA OFFERED HIM.

NOW I MUST LEAD HIM TOWARDS THE PALACE.

HE HASN'T EVEN NOTICED WE ARE NEAR THE PALACE.

ONCE HE WAS INSIDE THE PALACE, SANJAYA QUICKLY SHUT THE DOOR.

SLAM

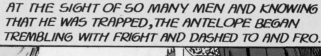

AT THE SIGHT OF SO MANY MEN AND KNOWING THAT HE WAS TRAPPED, THE ANTELOPE BEGAN TREMBLING WITH FRIGHT AND DASHED TO AND FRO.

WHEN THE KING CAME DOWN FROM HIS CHAMBER AND SAW THE ANTELOPE HE FELT SORRY FOR IT.

ANTELOPES ARE SO TIMID THAT THEY NEVER REVISIT A PLACE FOR AT LEAST A WEEK IF THEY HAVE SEEN A MAN THERE.

SOMETIMES THEY NEVER GO BACK AGAIN. THIS ANTELOPE WAS CARRIED AWAY BY THE TASTE OF THE SWEETENED GRASS AND FORGOT HIMSELF.

SURELY THERE IS NOTHING VILER IN THE WORLD THAN THE LUST OF TASTE. YOU HAVE TAUGHT US A VALUABLE LESSON.

GO MY FRIEND. YOU ARE FREE TO GO WHEREVER YOU PLEASE.

# *THE BANYAN DEER

IN TWO DIFFERENT PARTS OF A FOREST LIVED TWO HANDSOME GOLDEN STAGS. ONE WAS CALLED THE BANYAN DEER AND THE OTHER THE BRANCH DEER. EACH HAD A HERD OF ITS OWN.

NOW THE KING OF VARANASI WAS VERY FOND OF HUNTING DEER AND IN HIS LOVE OF IT HE DISTURBED ALL HIS TOWNSFOLK.

COME ON, EVERYONE, LET'S GO ON A HUNT.

ONE DAY THE PEOPLE GOT TOGETHER AND HIT UPON A PLAN.

LET US CHASE ALL THE DEER INTO THE KING'S GARDEN. THEN HE WILL NOT DISTURB US AT ODD HOURS TO GO INTO THE FOREST.

THEY GATHERED STICKS, POTS, PANS AND ANYTHING THAT MADE A NOISE TO DRIVE THE DEER INTO THE GARDEN.

* Based on Nigrodha Miga Jataka

28

THE NEXT DAY THEY SURROUNDED THE FOREST AND CHASED ALL THE DEER INTO THE KING'S GARDEN.

THERE! NOW HE WILL NOT DISTURB US WITH SO MANY DEER SO NEAR HIM.

BANG CLANG

A FEW TOWNSMEN WENT TO THE KING

SIR, YOU DISTRACT US FROM WORK WHEN YOU GO HUNTING; SO WE HAVE DRIVEN ALL THE DEER INTO YOUR GARDEN. SHOOT THEM WHENEVER YOU WISH.

AND SO THE KING WOULD GO OUT AND SHOOT DEER NOW AND AGAIN.

I MUST WARN MY MEN TO LEAVE THE GOLDEN STAGS ALONE.

SOMETIMES THE HEAD COOK WOULD ACCOMPANY HIM ON HIS HUNT.

LOOK, MY LORD! THERE GOES A PLUMP ONE.

NOT HIM. HE IS A GOLDEN STAG.

BUT THE DEER WERE BEING SLAIN IN SUCH LARGE NUMBERS THAT THE BANYAN DEER DECIDED TO DO SOMETHING ABOUT IT.

MY FRIEND, OUR DEER CANNOT ESCAPE DEATH BUT LET THEM NOT BE KILLED NEEDLESSLY. WE WILL SEND THEM TO THE BLOCK BY TURNS—ONE FROM MY HERD ONE FROM YOURS—EACH DAY.

IN THIS WAY THE DEER WHOSE TURN IT WAS WOULD GO TO THE BLOCK AND WAIT UP FOR THE COOK TO TAKE HIM AWAY.

HMMM, THIS IS A NICE PLUMP ONE TODAY.

ONE DAY IT WAS THE LOT OF A DOE WHO WAS ABOUT TO BE A MOTHER. SHE WENT TO THE BRANCH DEER.

MY LORD, LET ME ESCAPE THIS TIME. WHEN I HAVE HAD MY LITTLE ONE THERE WILL BE TWO OF US TO GO TO THE BLOCK.

NO, NO, I CANNOT DO THIS. GO AWAY.

SO SHE WENT TO THE BANYAN DEER AND TOLD HIM HER STORY.

VERY WELL. YOU DON'T GO THIS TIME. I WILL DO SOMETHING ABOUT IT.

HE HIMSELF WENT TO THE BLOCK THAT DAY.

WHEN THE COOK CAME ALONG HE WAS SURPRISED TO SEE ONE OF THE GOLDEN DEER AT THE BLOCK.

OH, OH! I MUST TURN BACK AND TELL THE KING.

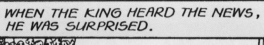

WHEN THE KING HEARD THE NEWS, HE WAS SURPRISED.

HE RUSHED TO THE SPOT.

WHY ARE YOU HERE? YOU ARE FREE TO LIVE.

YOUR MAJESTY, A DOE WHO WAS ABOUT TO BECOME A MOTHER CAME TO ME AND ASKED TO BE SPARED.

I HAVE COME IN HER PLACE. PLEASE SPARE HER.

THE KING WAS ASTOUNDED AT SUCH LOVE. HE WAS DEEPLY MOVED.

HE TURNED TO THE BANYAN DEER.

BOTH OF YOU SHALL LIVE. YOU DESERVE IT.

IF YOU CAN SPARE OUR LIVES, CAN'T YOU SPARE THE LIVES OF ALL THE DEER, YOUR MAJESTY?

I CAN! I WILL!

AND COULDN'T YOU SPARE THE LIVES OF ALL THE CREATURES IN YOUR FOREST, YOUR MAJESTY?

THE KING THOUGHT FOR A WHILE AND THEN—

ALL RIGHT! FROM THIS DAY, THERE SHALL BE NO HUNTING OR KILLING OF ANY KIND IN MY KINGDOM.

AND SO ALL THE ANIMALS IN THE FOREST LIVED IN PEACE AND HARMONY FOR A LONG TIME TO COME.

# ELEPHANT STORIES

## JATAKA TALES OF NOBILITY

**The route to your roots**

# ELEPHANT STORIES

An elephant's grace often matches his size. Amazingly patient and kind, he can put the petty greed of human beings to shame. But at times the odd elephant can turn nasty. What then can the smaller creatures of the world do to save themselves? Read the ancient wisdom of these Jataka tales to find out.

<table>
<tr><td>**Script**<br>Lakshmi Lal</td><td>**Illustrations**<br>Ashok Dongre</td><td>**Editor**<br>Anant Pai</td></tr>
</table>

*Cover illustration by: C.M.Vitankar*

## THE GREEDY FORESTER*

THE BODHISATTVA ASSUMED MANY FORMS THROUGH MANY LIFE CYCLES. AND SO IT WAS THAT WHEN BRAHMADATTA REIGNED IN VARANASI, HE WAS BORN AN ELEPHANT IN A FOREST IN THE HIMALAYAS.

HAVE YOU SEEN THE NEW BABY?

NOT YET. LET'S GO. I HEAR THAT HE IS BEAUTIFUL.

IN A GROVE OF DEODAR TREES, THE PROUD MOTHER STOOD, HER NEWBORN BY HER SIDE.

HE'S WHITE ALL OVER AND SHINES LIKE MOLTEN SILVER.

HE LOOKS LIKE A FULL MOON LEANING ON A DARK CLOUD.

* BASED ON SEELAVA NAGARAJA JATAKA

1

THE ELEPHANT GREW UP IN THE FOREST, WITH OTHER LITTLE ELEPHANTS.

LET'S SHAKE THIS BRANCH TO FRIGHTEN THE MONKEY ON IT.

WATCH ME SUCK THIS SQUIRREL INTO MY TRUNK.

AS HE GREW OLDER, HE NOTICED THAT MOST OF HIS COMPANIONS WERE SELFISH, GREEDY, EVEN CRUEL.

AAAH! AAAH!

THE WHITE ELEPHANT DECIDED TO LEAVE THE HERD.

I DON'T BELONG HERE. I'D RATHER LIVE ALONE.

AND SO HE DWELT APART, GIVING HELP AND GOOD COUNSEL WHEN NEEDED. ONE DAY HE SAW A LITTLE MONKEY WEEPING.

WHY ARE YOU CRYING?

I'M SMALL AND WEAK. MY FRIENDS TEASE ME.

HE GOT THE THOUGHT-LESS MONKEYS TO-GETHER.

SHAME ON YOU! WHY DO YOU HARASS YOUR WEAKER BROTHER, YOU WHO SHOULD PROTECT HIM? HAVE YOU NOT HEARD THE STORY OF···?

MANY AN EVENING FOUND HIM ADVISING AN EAGER GROUP OF ANIMALS, YOUNG AND OLD. SOON HE CAME TO BE KNOWN AS GOOD KING ELEPHANT.

ONE DAY, A FORESTER FROM VARANASI LOST HIS WAY IN THAT FOREST.

I HAVE NEVER FELT MORE FRIGHTENED IN MY LIFE. EVERY PATH SEEMS TO LEAD ME FARTHER AWAY FROM HOME.

WHY, HE SEEMS HARMLESS! HE'S ONLY FOLLOW-ING ME, NOT CHASING ME AS I THOUGHT.

EVERY TIME HE MOVED, THE ELEPHANT FOLLOWED. EVERY TIME HE STOPPED THE ELEPHANT TOO STOPPED.

I'LL TURN ROUND AND STOP. LET'S SEE WHAT HE DOES.

TO HIS SURPRISE, THE ANIMAL SPOKE TO HIM

I HEARD YOU SCREAM. IS THERE ANYTHING I CAN DO FOR YOU?

WHAT A KIND, GENTLE VOICE! AND YET, SO DEEP AND POWERFUL!

I'VE LOST MY WAY. I WANT TO GO TO VARANASI.

COME HOME WITH ME. I'LL GUIDE YOU TO THE CITY.

LATER, AT THE ELEPHANT'S CAVE —

YOU ARE EXHAUSTED. WHY DON'T YOU REST HERE FOR A FEW DAYS?

I THINK I WILL.

THE ELEPHANT'S DAY BEGAN EARLY.

I LIKE TO WATCH THE DAY BREAK OVER THOSE HILLS AS I BATHE.

IN THE EVENING THEY WALKED TO A CLEARING IN THE FOREST.

LET US WATCH THE SUN GO DOWN. IT FILLS MY HEART WITH PEACE.

I ENVY YOU, YOUR PEACE OF MIND. WE MEN ARE RESTLESS CREATURES.

AT THE EDGE OF THE FOREST, HE DISMOUNTED.

THERE LIES THE ROAD TO VARANASI.

THANK YOU, MY FRIEND.

AND REMEMBER, YOU MUST KEEP MY HAUNTS A SECRET FROM ALL MEN.

A FEW DAYS LATER, THE FORESTER HAPPENED TO VISIT THE IVORY BAZAAR AT VARANASI.

WHAT BEAUTIFUL THINGS YOU CREATE!

THEY COULD BE EVEN MORE BEAUTIFUL, BUT GOOD TUSKS ARE HARD TO COME BY.

ARE THEY? WOULD THE TUSK OF A LIVING ELEPHANT BE GOOD ENOUGH?

IT'S THE BEST, BUT IT'S RARE AND COSTS MUCH MORE THAN THE TUSK OF A DEAD ONE.

GREED GOT THE BETTER OF THE FORESTER. HE WENT BACK TO THE FOREST.

WHAT IS THE MATTER? YOU LOOK UNHAPPY.

I AM UP TO MY NECK IN DEBT. A PIECE OF YOUR TUSK CAN SAVE ME.

THE ELEPHANT SAT DOWN AND HELD HIS TRUNK OUT OBLIGINGLY.

I WILL GLADLY GIVE YOU BOTH MY TUSKS. BUT YOU WILL HAVE TO CUT THEM OFF.

I CAME PREPARED. I KNEW YOU WOULD NOT FAIL ME.

WHAT YOU HOLD ARE NO ORDINARY TUSKS. THEY ARE THE SOURCE OF ALL MY WISDOM.

BACK IN VARANASI, THE FORESTER RECEIVED A BIG SUM OF MONEY FOR THE TUSKS.

WHY, THERE IS MORE MONEY IN THIS THAN I THOUGHT! NOW I CAN BUY ALL THE SILKS AND JEWELS I WANT.

A MONTH LATER—

AFTER I BUY THESE THERE'LL BE NO MONEY LEFT. I SHOULD HAVE CUT CLOSER TO THE FLESH. WHAT A WASTE OF GOOD IVORY.

THAT NIGHT THE FORESTER COULD NOT SLEEP.

IF I CUT ANY MORE, THE ELEPHANT WILL SUFFER. BUT I MUST NOT BE SENTIMENTAL. I MUST GET HOLD OF THOSE PRECIOUS STUMPS OF TUSKS.

SO BACK HE WENT TO THE ELEPHANT. GREED HAD HARDENED HIS HEART.

YOUR TUSKS DID HELP TO CLEAR MY OLD DEBTS. BUT I NEED MORE MONEY IN ORDER TO LIVE.

YOU MAY HAVE WHAT IS LEFT OF MY TUSKS.

THE ELEPHANT CROUCHED DOWN TO GIVE THE TUSKS. THE MOMENT HAD COME FOR THE FORESTER TO CARRY OUT HIS CRUEL PLAN. HE PINNED THE ELEPHANT'S TRUNK DOWN WITH HIS FOOT, PULLED AT THE TUSKS...

...AND FINALLY SAWED THEM OFF.

NOW I HAVE DONE WITH YOU, MY FRIEND. I HAVE GOT ALL THERE IS TO GET.

AND HE WALKED AWAY, LEAVING THE ELEPHANT TORN AND TREMBLING. NOT A WORD OF REPROACH ESCAPED THE ELEPHANT'S LIPS.

SUDDENLY THE FORESTER FELT THE GROUND HEAVE UNDER HIS FEET. THE EARTH SPLIT OPEN AND A FIRE RAGED.

HELP! HELP!

THE FORESTER REALISED THAT HE WAS BEING PUN—ISHED FOR HIS GREED; BUT IT WAS TOO LATE.

AS THE FLAMES CONSUMED HIM, A VOICE WAS HEARD—

AN UNGRATE—FUL MAN IS NEVER SATISFIED— NOT EVEN IF HE IS GIVEN THE WHOLE WORLD.

AS FOR THE WISE ELEPHANT, HE LIVED THE REST OF HIS LIFE IN THE PEACE AND QUIET OF THE HIMALAYAS.

# THE BRAVE QUAIL*

IN A FOREST NEAR VARANASI, THERE ONCE LIVED SOME QUAILS. THE SHADY GROVE IN WHICH THEY NESTED WAS ALSO THE FAVOURITE GRAZING GROUND OF A HERD OF ELEPHANTS. A WISE AND JUST ELEPHANT, THE BODHISATTVA, WAS THE LEADER OF THAT HERD.

ONE DAY, ONE OF THE QUAILS LAID SOME EGGS.

I HOPE MY EGGS WILL BE SAFE TILL THEY ARE HATCHED.

YOU WILL HAVE TO KEEP CAREFUL WATCH. YOU KNOW HOW CARELESS THE ELEPHANTS ARE.

SOON THE FLEDGLINGS WERE HATCHED. ONE DAY—

LOOK! THE ELEPHANTS ARE MAKING FOR OUR GROVE!

WHAT SHALL I DO? I CAN ONLY FALL AT THEIR FEET AND BEG FOR PROTECTION.

* BASED ON LATUKIKA JATAKA

AS THE LEADER CAME CLOSE —

O MIGHTY ELEPHANT, MY LITTLE ONES ARE IN DANGER. IF YOUR HERD ENTERS THIS GROVE, THEY WILL BE TRAMPLED TO DEATH.

DO NOT FEAR. YOUR FLEDGLINGS WILL NOT BE HARMED.

THE ELEPHANT STOOD OVER THE NEST WHILE HIS HERD GRAZED. WHEN THEY HAD HAD THEIR FILL —

THERE IS A ROGUE-ELEPHANT, A WILD AND DANGEROUS ANIMAL, WHO MIGHT SOON BE COMING THIS WAY.

WHAT SHALL I DO? I AM SO SMALL AND WEAK.

YOU MUST APPEAL TO HIM FOR MERCY AND HOPE FOR THE BEST.

SOON AFTER THE ELEPHANTS HAD GONE —

THE ROGUE-ELEPHANT!

HE LOOKS FIERCE!

THE MOTHER QUAIL WASTED NO TIME. SHE WAS AT HIS FEET, HER HEAD LOWERED IN SALUTE.

HOW DARE YOU COME IN MY WAY?

O POWERFUL ONE, I BEG OF YOU, SPARE MY YOUNG ONES!

THE ELEPHANT LASHED AT THE NEST.

THERE! THAT IS THE END OF YOUR SILLY BROOD.

AS THE QUAIL WEPT OVER THE REMAINS OF HER DEAD CHILDREN—

I WILL SOON SHOW YOU HOW STRONG I AM!

GRIEF HAD MADE HER BOLD AND SET HER THINKING HARD. SHE WENT TO A CROW AND TOLD HIM HER SAD TALE.

YOU MUST SPOT THIS ROGUE-ELEPHANT AND PECK OUT BOTH HIS EYES.

DEPEND ON ME. SUCH WICKEDNESS SHOULD NOT GO UNPUNISHED.

HAVING GOT THE CROW ON HER SIDE, THE QUAIL WENT TO AN ANT.

MY LITTLE FRIEND, I NEED YOUR HELP.

I HEARD ABOUT YOUR BABIES. I AM DEEPLY GRIEVED.

THAT IS WHY I AM HERE. WE MUST TEACH THE CRUEL ELEPHANT A LESSON.

HOW CAN I HELP?

MY FRIEND THE CROW WILL PECK OUT HIS EYES. AFTER THAT YOU MUST LAY YOUR EGGS IN THE EMPTY SOCKETS.

A GOOD IDEA! WHEN THEY HATCH, MY LITTLE ONES WILL BEGIN TO BITE.

15

THE QUAIL THEN WENT TO THE FROG.

DEAR FRIEND, LEAVE EVERYTHING AND COME OUT!

THE FROG ROSE TO THE SURFACE AND CROAKED.

WHAT IS THE MATTER?

ALL MY YOUNG ONES WERE CRUELLY KILLED BY A SPITEFUL ELEPHANT.

I AM TRYING TO GET MY FRIENDS TO HELP ME PUNISH HIM.

YOU CAN COUNT ON ME.

AS THEY WENT ALONG, THE QUAIL UNFOLDED HER PLANS.

··· WHEN THE ANTS HATCH, THE ROGUE-ELEPHANT WILL BE BADLY STUNG. HE WILL RUN BLINDLY, LOOKING FOR WATER TO EASE HIS PAIN. THIS IS WHAT I WANT YOU TO DO···

A LITTLE LATER, THE CROW DARTED AT THE ELEPHANT...

... PLUCKED HIS EYES OUT. AND FLEW AWAY.

A-A-AH !

THEN, THE ANT LAID HER EGGS IN HIS BLIND EYES.

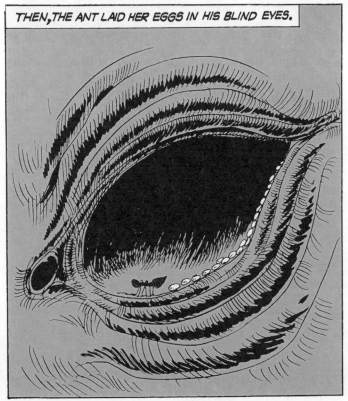

A-A-AH! MY EYES ARE ON FIRE. WATER! I NEED WATER!

JUST THEN THE FROG CROAKED FROM A STEEP PRECIPICE CLOSE BY.

CROAK

THE CROAK OF A FROG! THERE MUST BE WATER NEAR BY. I'LL FOLLOW THE SOUND.

AS THE ELEPHANT GOT TO THE EDGE OF THE PRECIPICE ...

CROAK

... THE FROG LEAPT ONTO A NARROW LEDGE BELOW AND CROAKED WITH ALL HIS MIGHT.

CROAK

THE ELEPHANT FOLLOWED THE SOUND AND WENT HURTLING DOWN TO HIS DEATH.

WHEN THE CROW, THE ANT, THE FROG AND THE QUAIL MET LATER —

I HOPE THE STORY OF THE ELEPHANT WILL BE A GOOD EXAMPLE TO ALL STRONG CREATURES WHO HARM THE WEAK AND THE HELPLESS.

# THE ROYAL ELEPHANT*

WHEN KING BRAHMADATTA REIGNED IN VARANASI, THERE LIVED, NOT FAR FROM THE CITY, A COLONY OF CARPENTERS.

EVERY DAY THEY WOULD SAIL DOWN THE RIVER AND ENTER A DENSE FOREST TO FELL TREES FOR TIMBER.

THUS THEY MOVED FROM FOREST TO VILLAGE AND BACK AGAIN. WORK WAS PLENTIFUL.

WE NEVER SEEM TO HAVE ENOUGH WOOD!

I NEVER SEEM TO HAVE ENOUGH TIME.

*BASED ON ALEENACHITTA JATAKA

ONE DAY, AS THEY SAT DOWN TO THEIR MIDDAY MEAL, THEY SAW AN ELEPHANT.

HE IS LIMPING AND SEEMS TO BE IN GREAT PAIN.

HE'S COMING TOWARDS US.

THE ELEPHANT CAME UP TO THE CARPENTERS AND HELD OUT A FOOT.

I STEPPED ON SOMETHING — I THINK IT'S A SPLINTER.

YOU ARE RIGHT. IT HAS ENTERED QUITE DEEP INTO THE FLESH.

THEY REMOVED THE SPLINTER, BATHED AND DRESSED THE WOUND AND NURSED THE FOOT BACK TO HEALTH.

YOU HAVE BEEN VERY KIND TO ME. I WOULD LIKE TO COME HERE EVERY DAY AND HELP YOU.

THE ELEPHANT SERVED THEM WELL FOR A NUMBER OF YEARS. ONE DAY —

LOOK! OUR FRIEND HAS BROUGHT A YOUNG ONE WITH HIM TODAY.

WHAT A BEAUTIFUL WHITE ANIMAL!

I AM NO LONGER AS ACTIVE AS I USED TO BE. I HAVE BROUGHT MY SON TO TAKE MY PLACE.

I WILL TRY MY BEST TO PLEASE YOU IN EVERY WAY.

THE YOUNG ELEPHANT WORKED HARD. HE HELPED TO LOAD AND UNLOAD TIMBER.

HE FETCHED AND CARRIED TOOLS...

...AND TRANSPORTED LOGS.

MORE, HE BROUGHT JOY AND LAUGHTER INTO THE CARPENTERS' LIVES FOR HE KEPT THEIR CHILDREN AMUSED.

OOOH! WHAT A LOVELY SWING!

ONE DAY, QUITE BY ACCIDENT, THE RAIN WASHED SOME OF HIS DROPPINGS INTO THE RIVER. LATER, DOWNSTREAM, WHERE THE ROYAL ELEPHANTS BATHED —

OUR ELEPHANTS ARE REFUSING TO GET INTO THE WATER.

LET US REPORT THE MATTER TO THE KING.

THE TRAINER GUESSED THE TRUTH.

THE WATER CONTAINS THE DROPPINGS OF A NOBLE ANIMAL. HE MUST LIVE UP-STREAM SOME-WHERE.

WHEN THE TRAINER REPORT-ED THE MATTER TO THE KING—

SCOUR THE COUNTRYSIDE. IF THERE IS SUCH AN ANIMAL HE SHOULD ADORN THE ROYAL STABLES.

THE KING HIMSELF SET OUT WITH A BAND OF TRUSTED MEN.

WITHIN MINUTES THEY TRACED THE ELEPHANT.

THAT MUST BE THE ANIMAL WE ARE LOOKING FOR. HOW NOBLY HE BEARS HIMSELF!

SOON —

THE KING!

DO YOU THINK HE WANTS US TO WORK IN THE PALACE?

IF HE DID, HE WOULD SEND FOR US, NOT COME HERE HIMSELF.

WHEN THE KING AND HIS PARTY DREW NEARER —

YOUR MAJESTY, WE ARE HONOURED. HOW CAN WE BE OF SERVICE TO YOU?

WE WOULD LIKE THIS ELEPHANT FOR OUR ROYAL STABLES.

THE ELEPHANT SEIZED THE OPPORTUNITY TO HELP HIS FRIENDS.

THESE MEN HAVE BEEN VERY KIND TO ME. I AM GREATLY INDEBTED TO THEM.

THE KING TURNED TO HIS MEN.

PAY THEM A HUNDRED THOUSAND PIECES OF GOLD FOR HIS TAIL, THE SAME FOR HIS TRUNK AND FOR EACH OF HIS FOUR FEET.

THE ELEPHANT WAS NOT SATISFIED.

YOU MUST NOT THINK ME GREEDY, YOUR MAJESTY. THEY NEED CLOTHES. AND THE CHILDREN TOO MUST BE PROVIDED FOR.

WE ADMIRE YOUR LOYALTY. WE SHALL MORE THAN SATISFY YOU.

UPON RECEIVING THIS ASSURANCE THE ELEPHANT AGREED TO GO WITH THE KING. IT WAS A SAD LEAVE-TAKING.

A KING'S COMMAND MUST BE OBEYED. YOU ARE GOOD CHILDREN AND WILL UNDERSTAND.

WHO WILL PLAY WITH US?

AND THE ELEPHANT LEFT FOR VARANASI WITH THE KING AND HIS MEN.

25

THE CITY WORE A FESTIVE AIR. THE ELEPHANT, REGALLY CAPARISONED, WAS LED TO HIS GAILY DECORATED STABLE.

THE NOBLES AND MINISTERS LOOKED ON IN ADMIRATION.

HE IS THE MOST MAJESTIC ANIMAL I HAVE EVER SEEN.

MARK MY WORDS! HE WILL PROVE HIS WORTH IN TIMES OF WAR.

THE KING MADE OVER HALF HIS KINGDOM TO THE ELEPHANT.

YOU ARE A BROTHER TO ME AND A COMPANION FOR LIFE.

THE ELEPHANT BECAME DEEPLY ATTACHED TO THE KING AND FOLLOWED HIM EVERY-WHERE.

MY LORD, HE REFUSES TO TOUCH HIS FOOD TILL YOU HAVE FIRST FED HIM A MORSEL.

A FEW MONTHS LATER, THE QUEEN WAS EXPECTING A BABY.

THE ELEPHANT HAS BROUGHT US GREAT GOOD FORTUNE. MY POWER AS A MONARCH IS NOW UNCHALLENGED.

I FEEL OUR CHILD IS DESTINED FOR GREAT THINGS.

BUT THEIR JOY WAS SHORT-LIVED. THE KING FELL SERIOUSLY ILL. AS HE LAY DYING—

MY ELEPHANT WILL BE BROKEN-HEARTED.

OUR CHILD WILL NEVER KNOW A FATHER!

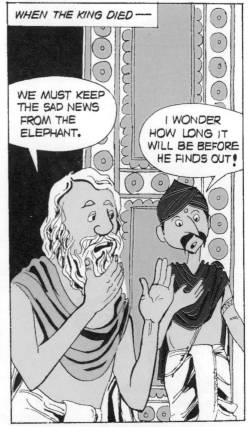

WHEN THE KING DIED—

WE MUST KEEP THE SAD NEWS FROM THE ELEPHANT.

I WONDER HOW LONG IT WILL BE BEFORE HE FINDS OUT!

MEANWHILE, THE KING OF KOSALA WAS MARCHING TOWARDS VARANASI.

THE KING IS DEAD, AND CONFUSION REIGNS.

THERE WERE HURRIED CONSULTATIONS AT VARANASI.

WE SHOULD ASK THEM TO SUSPEND FIGHTING FOR A WEEK.

HOW WILL THAT HELP?

ACCORDING TO THE ASTROLOGERS, THE QUEEN WILL GIVE BIRTH TO HER CHILD WITHIN A WEEK. IF IT IS A SON, WE WILL FIGHT. IF NOT, WE WILL SURRENDER.

THE KING OF KOSALA ACCEDED TO THEIR REQUEST.

A WEEK LATER —

LONG LIVE THE NEW-BORN KING!

FIGHT FOR THE KING! FIGHT TO THE LAST MAN!

THEY FOUGHT BRAVELY, BUT THE LACK OF LEADERSHIP TOLD ON THEM.

WE HAVE LOST HEAVILY.

WHAT DO YOU EXPECT? OUR LEADER LIES IN A CRADLE.

I HAVE AN IDEA. LET THE ROYAL ELEPHANT TAKE CHARGE.

THEY WENT TO THE QUEEN WHO SENT FOR THE ELEPHANT. WHILE HE GAZED AT HER SON—

HIS FATHER IS DEAD. IF THE KING MEANT ANYTHING TO YOU, HE IS NOW YOUR CHARGE.

THE KING DEAD! WHY WAS I NOT TOLD? HOW CAN I LIVE WITH-OUT MY MASTER?

...AND WHICH IS AT THIS VERY MOMENT IN GRAVE DANGER.

AS I DO, FOR HIS CHILD AND FOR THE KINGDOM THAT IS HIS BY RIGHT...

THE ELEPHANT KNELT TO RECEIVE THE QUEEN'S BLESSING.

I SHALL TALK NO MORE OF DEATH. YOUR SON SHALL RULE.

WE NOW HAVE SOMETHING TO LIVE FOR.

AS THE KEEPER OF THE ROYAL STABLES GOT HIM READY FOR THE BATTLE...

... THE KING'S MEN FELT THEIR HOPES RISE.

GET THE TROOPS OUT! LET NO MAN DAWDLE!

# A COLLECTOR'S EDITION,
# FROM INDIA'S FAVOURITE STORYTELLER.

India's greatest epic, told over 1,300 beautifully illustrated pages.
The Mahabharata Collector's Edition. It's not just a set of books, it's a piece of culture.

# THE MAHABHARATA
## COLLECTOR'S EDITION
*Rupees Two thousand, nine hundred and ninety-nine only.*

# JACKAL STORIES

## JATAKA TALES OF THE SLY AND THE SHREWD

**The route to your roots**

# JACKAL STORIES

The jackal has a bad reputation in the animal world. Devious, selfish, dishonest and boastful, his aspirations are high, but his talents few. He seldom repays a favour. Should such a creature be tolerated? Only so long as he uses his cunning for the good of the community, says the wisdom of these Jataka tales which were written as early as the period between 3rd century BC and 5th century AD.

**Script**
Kamala Chandrakant

**Illustrations**
Chandrakant Rane

**Editor**
Anant Pai

*Cover illustration by: C.M. Vitankar*

# THE JACKAL AND THE RATS

ONE DAY, WHILE ROAMING IN THE FOREST IN SEARCH OF FOOD, A JACKAL SUDDENLY SPIED A TROOP OF RATS. THEIR KING WAS A HUGE BANDICOOT.

I COULD ATTACK THEM. BUT THEN I'D CATCH ONLY ONE AND THE REST WOULD RUN AWAY.

IF I'M CLEVER, HOWEVER, THESE RATS COULD PROVIDE ME WITH FOOD FOR MANY DAYS.

SO HE FOLLOWED THEM TO THEIR HOLE.

WHEN THE LAST OF THEM HAD GONE INTO THE HOLE, THE JACKAL STOOD OUTSIDE ON ONE LEG, HIS MOUTH OPEN AND HIS FACE TURNED TOWARDS THE SUN.

1

HAIL, SAINTLY ONE.

HAIL!

HAIL!

THEIR WORSHIP OVER, THE RATS TROOPED AWAY...

...WHILE THE JACKAL SWIFTLY SWOOPED UPON THE LAST OF THEM.

THIS WENT ON FOR MANY DAYS. THEN THE BANDICOOT NOTICED SOMETHING.

FOR ALL HIS LIVING ON AIR, HOW PLUMP THIS SAINT HAS BECOME!

A LITTLE LATER—

LORD, THERE AREN'T AS MANY OF US AS THERE USED TO BE.

WHAT COULD THE REASON FOR THIS BE?

THE JACKAL HAS GROWN PLUMPER AND MY SUBJECTS FEWER! COULD THE JACKAL...? I'LL FIND OUT.

SO THAT EVENING AS THE RATS WERE READY TO SET OUT —

TODAY ALL OF YOU GO AHEAD. I'LL COME OUT LAST.

IF MY GUESS IS CORRECT, HE'LL POUNCE ON ME. I MUST BE READY.

THE NEXT MOMENT THE JACKAL SPRANG AT HIM...

...BUT MISSED.

SO THIS IS YOUR GAME! YOU RASCAL!

THE BANDICOOT DUG HIS TEETH INTO THE JACKAL'S THROAT AND KILLED HIM.

BACK CAME ALL THE OTHER RATS AND THEY HAD A GRAND FEAST.

# THE JACKAL AND THE LION

A HUNGRY JACKAL ONCE SUDDENLY CAME ACROSS A LION WHO WAS ON HIS WAY HOME.

WHAT DO YOU WANT?

I CANNOT HOPE TO ESCAPE. IT WOULD BE WISER TO PLAY HUMBLE.

MY LORD, PLEASE LET ME BE YOUR HUMBLE SERVANT.

ALL RIGHT.

WHAT LUCK! I'LL NEVER HAVE TO GO HUNGRY AGAIN.

FOLLOW ME.

WHEN THEY REACHED THE LION'S DEN—

YOUR WORD IS MY COMMAND, MY LORD.

IF YOU DO AS I TELL YOU, YOU WILL BE WELL FED.

YOU WILL GO TO THE TOP OF THE MOUNTAIN EACH DAY AND SEE IF THERE ARE ANY ANIMALS ROAMING IN THE VALLEY BELOW.

AND IF I SEE ONE, MY LORD?

YOU WILL COME AND TELL ME ABOUT IT. THEN YOU WILL SAY: "SHINE FORTH IN ALL YOUR MIGHT, MY LORD."

THEN, AFTER I'VE KILLED THE ANIMAL AND EATEN MY FILL, YOU MAY TAKE WHAT'S LEFT.

SO THE NEXT DAY THE JACKAL WENT TO THE MOUNTAIN TOP.

HE SPED BACK TO THE LION...

...AND FELL AT HIS FEET.

THE LION KILLED THE ELEPHANT...

...AND ATE HIS FILL.

NOW YOU MAY EAT THE REST.

AS THE DAYS WENT BY, THE JACKAL GREW FATTER AND FATTER.

BUT, ALAS! HE GREW LESS AND LESS HUMBLE. ONE DAY—

WHY SHOULD I LIVE ON LEFTOVER FOOD? I, TOO, AM A FOUR-FOOTED CREATURE! WHY WORK FOR THE LION WHEN I COULD KILL ELEPHANTS AND BUFFALOES FOR MYSELF?

AFTER ALL, THE LION ONLY GETS HIS STRENGTH FROM THE MAGIC PHRASE, "GO FORTH AND SHINE IN ALL YOUR MIGHT".

HE APPEALED TO THE LION.

MY LORD, I HAVE LIVED FOR TOO LONG ON WHAT YOU KILL. I WOULD LIKE TO EAT AN ELEPHANT I HAVE KILLED MYSELF.

THE LION WAS SILENT FOR A WHILE.

WHAT A FOOLISH IDEA! HE'LL BE KILLED HIMSELF!

THE JACKAL NIMBLY BOUNDED AWAY...

...ON THE TRAIL OF THE ELEPHANT.

I'LL CATCH HIM BY THE THROAT AND KILL HIM.

HE SPRANG AT THE ELEPHANT...

...BUT MISSED HIM.

THE PUZZLED ELEPHANT JUST WALKED OVER HIM...

...AND THAT WAS THE END OF THE FOOLHARDY JACKAL.

# THE CLEVER JACKAL

A GROUP OF ROGUES WERE ONCE HAVING A GRAND PARTY.

TOWARDS MIDNIGHT—

CAN I HAVE SOME MORE MEAT?

YOU CAN HAVE MORE WINE IF YOU LIKE, BUT THERE'S NO MEAT LEFT.

WHAT! NO MEAT! BUT I MUST HAVE SOME!

I'LL GO TO THE CHARNEL-GROVE, KILL A PROWLING JACKAL, AND BRING YOU ITS MEAT.

CLUB IN HAND, THE BRAGGART SWAGGERED OFF.

WHEN HE REACHED THE GROVE —

I'LL PRETEND I'M A CORPSE. THAT WILL ATTRACT JACKALS AND KEEP AWAY LIONS AND TIGERS.

WHEN A JACKAL COMES NEAR, I'LL KILL HIM WITH MY CLUB.

A LITTLE LATER, A PACK OF JACKALS CAME BY.

LOOK, THERE'S A CORPSE. COME ON!

WAIT! LET ME MAKE SURE WE'RE SAFE.

SNIFF! SNIFF!

THE SMELL OF A LIVING MAN! JUST AS I THOUGHT! HE IS ONLY PRETENDING TO BE DEAD.

JUST THEN HE NOTICED THE CLUB.

HE IS PROBABLY WAITING TO KILL ONE OF US.

WAIT HERE. I'LL TAKE CARE OF THE RASCAL.

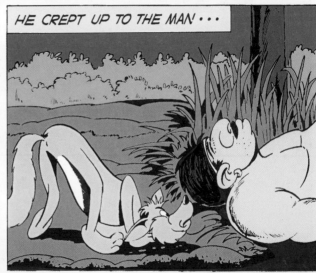

HE CREPT UP TO THE MAN···

···CAUGHT THE CLUB WITH HIS TEETH···

···AND GAVE IT A SLIGHT TUG.

IT MUST BE A BANDICOOT! I'D BETTER TIGHTEN MY GRIP.

THE NEXT MOMENT THE JACKAL LET GO OF THE CLUB WITH A JERK.

THE STARTLED ROGUE JUMPED TO HIS FEET, FLUNG HIS CLUB AT THE JACKAL · · ·

· · · AND MISSED!

I DARE NOT FACE MY FRIENDS AFTER MY VAIN BOAST.

I'D BETTER GO HOME AND SLEEP.

# THE JACKAL AND THE MAGIC SPELL

IN A SECLUDED SPOT IN A FOREST, THE FAMILY PRIEST OF BRAHMADATTA, KING OF VARANASI, WAS ONCE REPEATING A SECRET SPELL.

A JACKAL LYING NEAR BY PRICKED UP HIS EARS.

IF I LISTEN CAREFULLY I, TOO, CAN MASTER THAT.

A LITTLE LATER THE BRAHMAN GOT UP.

THERE! I'VE MASTERED IT.

THE NEXT MOMENT, TO HIS SURPRISE, A JACKAL STOOD BEFORE HIM.

HO! BRAHMAN, YOU COULDN'T HAVE MASTERED THE SPELL BETTER THAN I.

AND OFF HE RAN. THE PRIEST RAN AFTER HIM.

I MUST CATCH HIM! HE'LL PLAY HAVOC WITH THAT SPELL.

BUT THE JACKAL ESCAPED DEEP INTO THE FOREST.

I'LL FIRST GET MARRIED AND THEN, USING THE SPELL, I'LL BRING ALL THE FOUR-FOOTED CREATURES OF THE FOREST UNDER MY SWAY.

HE SOON FOUND HIMSELF A SHE-JACKAL.

IF YOU BECOME MY WIFE YOU SHALL BE QUEEN OF ALL THE ANIMALS OF THE FOREST.

I'M WILLING.

SNIFF SNIFF

LATER HE UTTERED THE SPELL AND ALL THE ANIMALS BEGAN TO FLOCK TOWARDS HIM.

YOU ARE OUR MASTER, O MIGHTY ONE!

YOU ARE OUR KING!

THEY SEATED THE JACKAL AND HIS WIFE ON A LION WHICH STOOD ON TWO ELEPHANTS.

THEY CONFERRED A TITLE ON THE JACKAL AND BOWED TO HIM.

HAIL!

HAIL SARVADATA, CHOSEN KING OF THE ANIMALS!

HAIL!

ALL THIS WENT TO THE JACKAL'S HEAD.

MY SUBJECTS, WE SHALL CAPTURE THE CITY OF VARANASI.

SO, WITH HIS GREAT FOLLOWING, HE MARCHED TO VARANASI.

WE SHALL CAMP HERE AND SEND A MESSAGE TO THE KING.

WHEN THE KING RECEIVED THE MESSAGE, HIS FAMILY PRIEST WAS WITH HIM.

"SURRENDER YOUR KINGDOM OR DIE FIGHT-ING FOR IT," HE SAYS.

HE HAS STRUCK TERROR EVERY-WHERE. HIS CAMP COVERS AN AREA OF THIRTY-SIX MILES! WHO IS THIS ANIMAL?

HE IS SARVADATA, THE JACKAL-KING. LEAVE HIM TO ME. I'LL FIND A WAY OF DEFEATING HIM.

ALL RIGHT. MAY YOU BE SUCCESSFUL.

I MUST FIRST FIND OUT WHAT HE INTENDS TO DO.

O SARVADATA, HOW DO YOU PLAN TO TAKE THIS CITY?

I WILL MAKE THE LIONS ROAR AND CREATE PANIC AND CHAOS AMONG THE PEOPLE. THEN I WILL MARCH INTO THE CITY.

OH! SO THAT'S IT!

IMPOSSIBLE! THESE NOBLE CREATURES WILL NEVER OBEY A COMMON JACKAL.

THAT'S WHAT YOU THINK! THE LIONS WILL ALL OBEY ME. EVEN THIS LION ON WHOSE BACK I SIT WILL ROAR.

DON'T BRAG. GET HIM TO ROAR — IF YOU CAN.

OBEY YOUR KING! ROAR WITH ALL YOUR MIGHT!

GRR-R R!
GRR-R-R!

THE LION ROARED AND ROARED. TERRIFIED, THE ELEPHANTS SHOOK OFF THE LION. THE JACKALS CRASHED TO THE GROUND.

SEEING THE ELEPHANTS RUN AMUCK, ALL THE ANIMALS BROKE INTO A STAMPEDE AND RAN HELTER SKELTER.

IN THE STAMPEDE, THE JACKALS WERE TRAMPLED TO DEATH.

THAT WAS THE END OF KING SARVADATA WHO HAD DARED TO DREAM OF CONQUERING VARANASI.

# THE JACKAL AND THE OTTERS

A JACKAL'S WIFE ONCE WANTED TO EAT SOME FRESH ROHITA FISH. PROMISING TO BRING IT FOR HER, THE JACKAL WENT TO THE RIVER.

I'VE PROMISED TO BRING HER THE FISH. BUT HOW AM I GOING TO DO IT?

JUST THEN HE SAW TWO OTTERS DRAGGING ALONG A HUGE ROHITA FISH.

THIS FISH SHOULD LAST US A LONG TIME.

WHAT'S THE MATTER, FRIENDS?

THIS FISH WAS CAUGHT BY BOTH OF US. WE CANNOT DECIDE HOW TO DIVIDE IT.

WILL YOU DO IT FOR US?

JUST AS I EXPECTED!

CERTAINLY! YOU CAN LEAVE IT TO ME. I'VE SETTLED MANY CASES BEFORE AND SETTLED THEM FAIRLY.

THE JACKAL THEN CUT OFF THE HEAD AND THE TAIL OF THE FISH.

YOU TAKE THE HEAD···

# THE JACKAL AND THE SHE-GOAT

LONG AGO, IN A CAVE ON THE SLOPES OF THE HIMALAYAS, THERE LIVED A HERD OF WILD GOATS. ONE DAY, AS A JACKAL AND HIS MATE WERE PROWLING ABOUT FOR FOOD, THEY SAW THE GOATS GRAZING.

COME! LET US KILL ONE OF THEM.

WAIT! IF WE ARE CLEVER, WE'LL HAVE FOOD ENOUGH FOR MANY MONTHS.

THEY WAITED TILL THE GOATS BEGAN TO WANDER APART AS THEY GRAZED.

LET'S FOLLOW THAT ONE TILL HE IS FAR AWAY FROM THE OTHERS.

A FEW HOURS LATER —

THERE! I'VE KILLED HIM. NOW HELP ME DRAG HIM TO OUR CAVE.

MANY MONTHS PASSED AND, ONE BY ONE, THE GOATS WERE EATEN BY THE JACKALS.

THE ONLY ONE LEFT WAS A WISE SHE-GOAT.

I DARE NOT GO OUT. THE JACKALS ARE ABOUT AGAIN!

THAT SHE-GOAT SEEMS TO BE WISE TO US. SHE DOES NOT COME OUT AT ALL.

THE JACKAL HAD AN IDEA.

YOU GO ALONE EVERY DAY AND TRY TO WIN HER CONFIDENCE. WHEN SHE BEGINS TO TRUST YOU I WILL LIE OUTSIDE OUR CAVE AND PRETEND TO BE DEAD. AND YOU... BZZ. BZZ....

I AM VERY UNHAPPY. NO ONE IS WILLING TO BE MY FRIEND, BECAUSE OF MY HUSBAND'S EVIL WAYS.

THE KIND-HEARTED GOAT FELT SORRY FOR THE SHE-JACKAL.

PLEASE DON'T SAY THAT. I'LL BE YOUR FRIEND.

AS EACH DAY PASSED THE SHE-GOAT'S TRUST IN THE JACKAL INCREASED, TILL ONE DAY—

TOMORROW WE SHALL CARRY OUT THE NEXT PART OF OUR PLAN.

THE NEXT DAY—

OH, I AM LEFT ALL ALONE! MY HUSBAND IS DEAD. PLEASE COME AND HELP ME BURY HIM.

NO! NO! I CANNOT COME. I'M AFRAID OF HIM.

BUT WHAT HARM CAN HE DO TO YOU NOW THAT HE IS DEAD?

DEAD OR ALIVE, HE'S CRUEL AND I'M AFRAID TO COME OUT.

AND I HAD THOUGHT YOU WERE MY FRIEND! HOW UNFORTUNATE I AM THAT I MUST BURY MY HUSBAND ALL BY MYSELF!

SHE CAN'T BE LYING. HE MUST REALLY BE DEAD.

DON'T WEEP, MY FRIEND. I'LL COME WITH YOU.

AS THEY WERE ABOUT TO SET OUT, HOWEVER, THE SHE-GOAT SUDDENLY BECAME DOUBTFUL AGAIN.

FRIEND, YOU WALK AHEAD AND SHOW ME THE WAY. I'LL FOLLOW.

A LITTLE LATER—

AH, FOOTSTEPS! HERE THEY COME.

HE FORGOT THAT HE WAS SUPPOSED TO PLAY DEAD, AND OPENED HIS EYES TO LOOK AT THE PLUMP GOAT.

HE'S ALIVE!

THE WICKED WRETCH WANTS TO KILL ME. THEY ARE BOTH TRAITORS!

WHEN SHE HAD GONE —

HUMPH! I THOUGHT YOU HAD WON HER CONFIDENCE!

I HAD! BUT YOU, MY LORD, HAD TO BE A FOOL AND SPOIL IT ALL.

THE JACKAL WAS SO CRESTFALLEN THAT HIS MATE FELT SORRY FOR HIM.

DON'T LOOK SO UNHAPPY! I'LL BRING HER AGAIN. THIS TIME, BE ON YOUR GUARD.

AH! MY FRIEND, YOU HAVE PERFORMED A MIRACLE! AS YOU CAME NEAR HIM, MY HUSBAND CAME TO LIFE AGAIN. HE WANTS TO MEET YOU AND THANK YOU.

THE TRAITOR! SHE TAKES ME TO BE A TRUSTING FOOL. I'LL TEACH HER A LESSON SHE'LL NEVER FORGET!

THE SHE-GOAT CAME OUT.

ALL RIGHT, I'LL COME — WITH AN ESCORT OF TWO THOUSAND DOGS. IF THEY DO NOT FIND ENOUGH FOOD, THEY WILL DEVOUR YOU AND YOUR MATE. SO HURRY HOME AND PREPARE ENOUGH FOOD FOR US ALL!

THE RUSE WORKED.

TWO THOUSAND DOGS! I'VE HAD ENOUGH OF THIS GOAT.

DEAR FRIEND, I'VE CHANGED MY MIND. YOU'D BETTER NOT COME. YOUR CAVE MIGHT BE BURGLED WHILE YOU ARE AWAY.

BUT I WANT TO COME AND····

NO! PLEASE DON'T BOTHER. SOME OTHER TIME, PERHAPS.

THEN SHE RAN FOR HER LIFE···

···TILL SHE REACHED HER MATE.

QUICK! WE MUST RUN. OR ELSE WE'LL MAKE A MEAL FOR TWO THOUSAND DOGS!

TWO THOUSAND DOGS!

THE JACKAL AND HIS MATE TOOK TO THEIR HEELS. AND THEY WERE NOT SEEN OR HEARD OF EVER AGAIN.

# Mystique, Adventure and Magic

**MRP ₹180/-**

Amar Chitra Katha brings to you a unique collection of tales about magical beasts from the vast spectrum of Indian mythology and folklore. From Jatayu's valiant confrontation with Ravana to Nandi's unparalleled devotion to Lord Shiva, the book takes you on a fun ride across fascinating tales.

To buy this product, visit your nearest bookstore
or buy online at **www.amarchitrakatha.com** or call: **022-49188881/2**